Big Bing

by Andrea Patel
illustrated by Kersti Frigell

Core Decodable 52

McGraw Hill Education

Bothell, WA • Chicago, IL • Columbus, OH • New York, NY

MHEonline.com

Send all inquiries to:
McGraw-Hill Education
8787 Orion Place
Columbus, OH 43240

ISBN: 978-0-02-133597-8
MHID: 0-02-133597-4

Printed in Canada.

9 10 11 12 KOD 24

It is spring.
But Big Bing is still resting.

Bing must get up.
Will a long ring get Bing up?

A long ring will not do it.
Will a song do it?

Singing will not get Bing up.
Will banging do it?

Banging will not.
But hitting a big gong will.

Hitting a big gong did it.
Big Bing is up!